Maelstrom Origami

Also by Steve Spence

A Curious Shipwreck, Shearsman Books, 2010
Limits of Control, Penned in the Margins, 2011

Anthologies

In the Presence of Sharks, Phlebas, 2006
Orphans of Albion, Survivors Press/The Sixties Press, 2008
The Forward Book of Poetry, Forward Press, 2011
Smartarse, Knives, Forks and Spoons Press, 2011
Adventures in Form, Penned in the Margins, 2012
The Robin Hood Book, Caparison, 2012

Steve Spence

Maelstrom Origami

Shearsman Books

First published in the United Kingdom in 2014 by
Shearsman Books
50 Westons Hill Drive
Emersons Green
BRISTOL
BS16 7DF

Shearsman Books Ltd Registered Office
30–31 St. James Place, Mangotsfield, Bristol BS16 9JB
(this address not for correspondence)

www.shearsman.com

ISBN 978-1-84861-354-6

Acknowledgements

Some of these poems have previously been published in *Stride* magazine (online) and in *Tears in the Fence*.

Contents

I A Point of Entry

II Present Continuous

III The Manufacture of Desire

IV Bandits

V Moving in the Right Direction

For Hilary and for Keith
and in memory of
Florence May Spence,
1920-2014

I

A Point of Entry

Let us imagine someone who has encountered
the word 'chair' and does not know what it means.
Tonight there will be a magic lantern show.

Even in exile he was no longer safe yet there is
no simple correlation between colour and language.
Even basic typographical questions remain unsolved.

Beardless again, he looked even younger. For those
with a neurotic predisposition, the fear of dependency
may evolve into terror. Here too, we have a sentence.

A power balance is always delicate and can easily
be disrupted yet a man lying down is a man disarmed.
Are we semi-detached from the flow of time?

When the initial sounds had been achieved she started
to bring in the musicians. Are we semi-detached from
the flow of time? Later we may provoke a storm.

He lay with his head in the grass, staring at the parting
clouds. Speech perception is a highly active process.
After darkness came, the capital remained tense and edgy.

Have you ever roared with laughter in an empty room?
First there will be a greeting, followed by an interrogation.
They may be ungainly on land but puffins are superb divers.

As the months turn to years forgetting a fact can be seen
as disbelieving it. Once again I felt a lurch of fear. Condors
were found foaming at the beak and crashing into rocks.

What about a pink oyster mushroom?
Once again I felt a lurch of fear.

When does a stream become a river or a hill a
mountain? You may need to have your feet on the
ground and your head in the clouds at the same time.

Are you struggling to see the main stage? In the
final session, two experimenters were involved.
Communication is evidently a complex affair.

The police truck stopped and we were ordered to
get out. During reading, the eyes do not follow
lines of print in a smooth, linear manner.

"The important thing is that the painting's there,
nailed to the wall," she said. Are you using nuanced
language to underline your subliminal message?

We were aided by the fact that it was a very windy day.
Yet there are other ways of talking to the past and
life inside the compound is relatively pleasant.

Do we compete or do we collaborate? Yet it's important
to keep the momentum going and the longer they
pretend to pay us the longer we'll pretend to work.

"There is likely to be a zigzag pattern," he said.
Here the chief anxiety relates to the use of language
to convey the truth. To enter you must accept our rules.

Are you fascinated by conversation? Yet no
interaction is deemed to have happened unless
somebody has taken a picture of it.

Why can't we confine our mistakes to paint and canvas?
Silence is one way of shutting down a sensitive subject.

You could sense dampness in the air but no water.
When we reached the rocks I found several mackerel
hanging from the hooks.

Do you have any knowledge of anatomy? As the wind
changes the bats turn south and a network of associations
are built up between sounds.

Some sea slugs ooze poison yet there is a complex crossover
between eating and hunting. Grammatical handicaps are
shown by a restrictive range of sentence construction.

It's a long, hot afternoon and we're stuck in the traffic.
A child is sitting opposite the experimenter. Elephants,
like cattle and deer, are often involved in road accidents.

She had drifted into his radar and he had locked on.
Of special note are the thimble jellyfish. A struggle
ensued with several people coming to her aid.

Most food-swap events last about two hours yet so much
of what we do is 'virtual' these days and none of these
birds have been trained. Hot-desking is not on our agenda.

Another surprising aquatic danger is the snapping turtle
and the context of an attack is always important. The only
downside seems to be a lack of humour in her work.

When there is temptation someone will always succumb,
yet these skills are not necessarily transferable, and we now
have a listener telling us about his life as a mystery shopper.

In flight, the nightjar is almost as big as the
kestrel yet victims often disappear without a noise.

When will the work begin? He immediately set
about adding his full range of talents to the song.
I'd like to tell you about the story that never was.

"We need a one-off amnesty with stronger border
controls," she said. This is a young country where
the pace of change can be very fast.

These skills are not necessarily transferable yet
beckoning can be carried out with the palm of the hand.
The patience of a crocodile can last for weeks.

Is it true that you hate being touched? Yet some
research focuses on the problem of feedback and
different plants demand different methods of collection.

Most people in the west will eat shrimps but not
insects. At the same time there are groups of riot
police who are relaxing, leaning on their shields.

"I absolutely insist that we use live musicians",
she said. She is intrigued by everything about
their behaviour. After his victory he glistened with sweat.

These cuts are just the next phase in an ongoing
process yet another big problem arises out of the
use of abbreviation. This is a predominantly poor community.

Often, with these things, there's a dynamic of bloodshed
yet this whole area acts as a filter for what is coming off
the land. "As a student of language, it has to be the OED" he said.

She is intrigued by everything about their behaviour, from
the clothes they wear to their social-networking habits.

Let's start with some statistics. Everyone thinks they are
under attack in cyberspace yet humans have increasingly
knocked down traditional barriers between land and sea.

As I remembered this unusual set of facts, a wasp
crawled into my ear. The colours warmed and deepened
as he watched. "We've decided to let you go," she said.

Attribution can be very hard yet these attacks have
become consistently ingenious, seeking flaws in the
supply chain. Pollinators are on the decrease.

Are we making marine life ill with human diseases?
Above all, it's the look that he catches in the faces of
his women. Welcome to the maelstrom.

If these images are widely shared we don't know in whose
hands they might end up. Yet the real price of an object is
not what it costs to buy but what it costs to make.

Not all desire is greed but are we now indifferent to the
notion of justice for all? Some birds defend themselves
not by fighting but by stinking.

What we have here are fermenting carrots. There is
something a bit retro about a foot spa but that is no reason
not to have one. On the other shelf is an array of vinegars.

We passed high fences, tipped with razorwire.
Surely we could draw borders that would make
more sense. Naked, she took his breath away.

Captivity changes things. Now people cross over
the street to avoid me. Are you anxiously attached?

"I like the action of a real piano" she said.
How much information were you given by the director?
Yet the song of the blackbird has a seductive quality.

There may be no simple choice between economy and
ecology yet cooking is still done over an open fire. As he
was adjusting his camera, the beast revived and charged.

"If we've got to go out let's go out with a bang," he said.
Small species are always collected in larger quantities from
a single locality. It's important to get independent advice.

She is more the anthropologist looking in from a distance
than she is the gossip columnist. The roofs of their mouths
are lined with short teeth and curve back towards the throat.

His testimony effectively put an end to the trial yet the forces
of law and order were equally complicit and partisan.
Throughout history, shipwrecks have turned people into prey.

In a nutshell, what pleased you most about this recent win?
There is a seedy glamour about absinthe yet one glass per
session is a sensible option. You're never alone with a radio.

In changing our behaviour, do we change what we are?
This new type of surface coating is so slick that it can
make molasses slide like olive oil. "It rankles still."

It was not nausea that hit me so much as indignation.
What we're getting now is a row over numbers yet fossil
evidence suggests otherwise. Cheaper drinks could be to blame.

Can great-feeling skin change your body language?
How do we keep sane under such a deluge of information?

Nobody chooses the cacophony of different channels, do they?
Micro-organisms remain the basis of the main food system yet
this outward process mirrors the inward process of going to sleep.

What happens when you start to talk about nature in an economic
context? At the heart of this campaign is the catchiest song you'll
hear in a long time. During my spell on the tills I witnessed all of life.

Sometimes the impulse to surrender can be contaminated with the
need for self-punishment. Here, lava flows have constructed a city of
monstrous arches. Two chunks of the fish's beak remained in his neck.

A name synonymous with showmanship and extravagance, he was
a performer with flair. Here we have a dazzling kaleidoscope of colour.
A few men had life rafts but these were no guarantee of safety.

One approach is 'bottom-up', directed self-assembly yet we also focus
on the most important thing, which is taste. The Humboldt squid grows
to six feet and weighs more than twenty five pounds.

You should keep a low profile or your approach could flush the birds.
I'm sorry but I can't tell you exactly where I've been today. Then he
was off, ignoring us for long stretches, as if to keep us guessing.

"When I was a young man, I was a fan of permanent revolution,"
he said. Cognition is complex and whether it looks like a Swiss army
knife or a giant amoeba may depend on what aspect we are studying.

Even fish and shellfish established as edible sometimes prove
poisonous yet here we have an economy in freefall. Absinthe is
also said to be a short-term stimulant to memory.

When I was a young man I played the amusement halls.
Are these growing pains or are we in a state of stagnation?

For the vast majority of people, gambling is a leisure pursuit.
Are you or have you ever been a member of a proscribed
organisation? "We did wonder, when you ordered so much food."

There's no excuse not to hear the music. Even so, the omens for
long-term success don't look good. In certain cases, some plants
require special treatment before drying.

Statements about a lack of provocation are always problematic.
Yet it's best to avoid collecting specimens during hot weather.
We need to be extensively engaged with gathering information.

It often feels to me as if things get lost in translation. If anything,
these welfare reforms will only push people deeper into poverty.
Welcome to the Azores where even the fish look extra-terrestrial.

Whether it happens or not, the temptation for intelligence
services to exploit mismatches in national laws is beyond doubt.
These aggressive predators possess folding claws like jack-knives.

How do you balance scientific discourse with character development?
At this time of year the mind begins to wander. Once again it was a
mouse that was bugging him. Where you get nutrients you get plankton.

It's always difficult to select suitable candidates for public office
but these are carnivores, licking the flesh from their prey with their
toothed tongues. We were hoping for a different kind of storm.

Have you ever drunk the syrup of beech trees? There is also a
short film, in which the couple are shown getting dressed. Finally,
everything is secured by straps and placed in a warm, dry place.

He broke down in tears before answering
the question for the first time in his career.

Here, under the warmth of the sun, vineyards blanket
a hilly landscape. Are you feeling threatened by the
underclass? A drab appearance may hide a colourful life.

"We're losing eye-to-eye contact", he said. As for the
ethics of killing one species to protect another, the professor
is unapologetic. It's fairly difficult to get bitten by a rattlesnake.

This may prove to be the most spectacular wildlife experience
of your life. At which point we saw a rise in products and a
consequent rise in consumer society.

Have you ever experienced conger eel soup? Everything
comes down to how we cope with change. "Yes but why do
we have to listen to Steve Wright in the afternoon", asked Luke.

There are threats and then there are opportunities.
Are you a cultural entrepreneur or a taste-shaper?
"I was unaware I was being recorded", she said.

Many are spider specialists and lure their prey
by mimicking the movement of trapped insects.
There is, for example, the hairy alpine rose.

Let's deal with economic espionage first. Yes, but
it's usually violence that makes people concentrate
on why politics is the best form of government.

A large, undefined frame of red seems to hover in front of a
maroon background. "We may be able to help you think about
thinking", she said. The bite of a crocodile is rich with bacteria.

We must break down your text
and subject it to vigorous analysis.

Great arcs of paint cover the canvas, apparently at
random, to produce an intense and energetic abstract
plane. Once again, the room is filled with eager pirates.

Victims often disappear without even making a noise.
Are you trying to stitch me up? Yet there's a typewriter
lying on the floor and it's covered in dust.

"I wanted to record neighbours being neighbours",
she said. They shift and change with the fluidity of
the times. Each click is like a dim camera flash.

In the last analysis it's the analysis that's causing trouble.
Yet the curators are calling this an 'immersive' exhibition
and woe betide anything that gets caught in the surface film.

While crawling around to feed, the kissing bug
defecates on the skin of sleeping people. They usually
have jobs and attend training sessions in their own time.

Which sort of conversation would you most like
to study? Yet the existence of advanced surveillance
technologies suggest we are in new territory.

Under questioning he could usually recall minor events
shortly before the time of his operation. Was his case
responsible for sparking an interest in conversation analysis?

It may not be okay to share these images but a baitball might
only last for ten minutes before being wiped out. Which sort
of conversation would you most like to study?

Let's talk about the effects of postcode profiling. Are we
responsible for sparking an interest in conversation analysis?

Having a beard does not make you a philosopher
yet the question of bait remains an open one.
There may also be an environmental impact.

Each position will carry with it certain linguistic
conventions. How well do you function in an
open-plan office space?

Whole dynasties have been built on this kind
of fixation yet a habitable environment always
includes three important ingredients.

Sometimes it pays not to translate. "It's a communal
kitchen, obviously", she said, yet visual effects
often interact specifically with speech.

People find the lack of privacy difficult yet this
is a beautiful stretch of water and perfect silence
may not be the answer either.

In the folklore of the sea we find many monsters
with a multiplicity of tentacles and snaky necks.
Each species has special environmental requirements.

What sort of brutality had they learned to absorb
in growing up? Most of the government checkpoints
have disappeared but we don't have to kill our prey.

"I've never had a real job and I don't want one
now", he said. Can we live longer and consume less?
There is also the question of intellectual property.

Even as I type these words I wonder what
processes are going on in my over-active brain.

This species is fairly aggressive and will occasionally
bite if handled. Can we take orders from a machine?
In most cases, puzzle-solvers are made, not born.

You can't just go around recording people or
can you? What's really going on behind the headlines?
If we succeed they will turn green and flourish.

While he usually rules the roost he is no longer
comfortable around hoodies yet this is a typical
example of miscommunication between species.

"Maybe these offices look good but they don't help
us to concentrate", she said. At this point their fragile
agreements were strained to breaking point.

"You can't experiment for ever and I work very slowly",
she said. Overlapping squares and rectangles of textured
and mottled paper are juxtaposed on a round board.

In this case, both hook and bait should be smaller
than those used on a paternoster rig. Even now, there
is little academic research on neighbourhood disputes.

Communication of information may be marginal to the process
of conversation yet the little egret may now appear in your
back garden. Overall, the tour went down as an artistic success.

For me, the cattle grid is like a found musical object.
Other processes have involved burning a canvas, stepping
on paint or dripping water onto a surface.

"We are committed to transparency", he said. Yes,
but what is causing the jet stream to shift in this way?

After breakfast the ducks have to take care of
themselves for the rest of the day. According to
this report it looks like you're going off the radar.

There is a theory that the 'sleep room' was not
a treatment centre at all yet I had no idea that
anyone could possibly be living there now.

The greater the amplitude, the greater the
intensity of the sound. They are a shy animal
and are more shy of us than we are of them.

In many cases, the linguistic characteristics of
social roles are fairly easy to identify, yet Kate's
electronic experiments are all over the album.

They filmed in long-shot and we see them through
the glass walls as if they are exotic animals. What
does a composer bring to the sounds of the city?

If you've got a lot of mouths to feed this extra-large
machine will come in handy. It's four o'clock in
the morning and I'm off to meet the sound artist.

You can spend hours examining the way he
depicts light falling on a viola but a decent
pair of scissors doesn't have to break the bank.

Usually everyone goes home with a good haul, yet as
the title states, this is not a straightforward self-portrait
and only young shoots should be used for this purpose.

An unnamed senior officer is said to have signed off the
secret tapes and we advise you not to answer this question.

As with any structure, the whole cannot be
broken down into its constituent parts without
loss, yet many offices have internal windows only.

Is it back to the dark days of butter mountains and
wine lakes? Accelerating technology has eroded
our right to privacy but of course the train was late.

"We were brought up to believe that the state
would only do us harm", she said. We splashed
through the dark lobby to a door under the stairway.

When he had finished I ran my index finger around
the plate a few times yet swimming is banned and these
figures are shown simultaneously from a range of angles.

His answers were long and rambling and it's important
to work out exactly what went wrong. "These weapons
are only used for defensive purposes", he said.

This may prove to be a game-changer yet the
politics of the street moves very fast and several
factors may prompt a crocodile to attack.

As any parrot owner will tell you, a pet bird can
give you a serious bite. As we watched, the crater
just got bigger and bigger. Just look at that fish go.

Somehow these cameras have become best-sellers
yet far away from earth it makes more sense to
work with sun-relative measurements.

"I don't believe in arms, I believe in negotiations",
he said. "It's high time for diplomacy".

Red lines radiate from a wound like the spokes of a
wheel. This may provide effective protection against
predators. Also amazing for its voracity is the bluefish.

Translating research findings into clear dietary
recommendations will prove a challenge. There's
always hope as long as you've got a bait in the water.

Early harvesting may prove disastrous yet
this is espionage on an industrial scale.
One robot thought itself to be an expert welder.

For the full effect, stand as close to the front of
the arena as you possibly can. There will always
be a chance that a few rats will survive the cull.

Are we doomed to keep experiencing these
emotions? I could hear the slight pause when
she turned each page of manuscript, then silence.

For a while there was a sense of genuine democracy
in the air. Surfers are the most frequent victims yet
close observation reveals only the usual bisexual flowers.

A wall is positioned in front of a window at the far
end of a room. Significant differences appear yet he
is also well-known for his large, mural decorations.

Why have they left no clear archaeological record?
As you've probably gathered, the Talmud is no ordinary
book yet the object of the exercise is to put people over fish.

A city is much more than its buildings and people.
One by one the sharks disappear.

II

Present Continuous

"I didn't want to spend my life in an office", he said.
"I felt I was different". There is no compelling evidence
here yet in the fireplace the gas hisses with a blue flame.
We are in a state of confusion. Do not open the window.
The bombardment will carry on until the shoal manages to
escape downwards. Are we greater than the sum of our parts?
This may also depend on what you measure velocity relative
to yet they use their bony bills to slash their prey. We can't
breathe and we can't see the sky. Are we talking about
appeasement here or caution? Sound, of course, is very
important in the life of birds. Experts agree that the risk of
human infection remains low. "Yet I have never, ever been
happier in my life", he said. There is no military solution to
this situation. Are we talking about appeasement or caution?

Are the new security costs an unavoidable price to pay for our economic stability? Yet we wanted to be sure that these policies would be carried out. Five seconds later the screen went blank. "I've never seen human beings so destitute and so hopeless", she said. A number of us who were there that night are here now. This is when the fish come in to play. You meet all kinds of people here, some you know, some you don't. We tumble into the rubble of the interior of the house, sending up small spurts of dust. Since opening, business has been brisk. Cream and white are the obvious choice for purists. "It's a very simple, light-detecting task", she said. Is this an innovative lie to cover up a night out? At this point in time marine fish and deepwater species are becoming very common. Instead, it became a model for privatised war and reconstruction. This is when the fish come in to play.

How do you know we don't already know the numbers?
None of this seems conducive to concentration yet in the
summer we migrate to very deep water for spawning.
Your timetable seems unclear. Is this going to be a short,
sharp shock? Yet woe betide those who seek to present a
nuanced view. Fortunately, several intermediate positions
seem to be emerging. When you make strange noises here
(sea) birds fall from the sky. In less than an hour this proved
to be all too true yet the yard remains stacked with vital
stores and equipment. The ground will be frozen to a depth
of one hundred yards to try and prevent radioactive water
from spreading more widely. Are you engaged online?
In a heap of junk outside the shack I found a rusted chisel.
There is still no sign of an enemy.

What should we make of these results? Deliberately pushing your opponent is disallowed yet it's an arena of conflict with sharply defined rules and everybody is leaving the area. Is this the direction in which we are headed? There is no second building. There is panic in the streets. There are reported cases of deer bursting through windows into houses, possibly confused by reflections. There is panic in the streets. Sometimes this drug may induce feelings of schadenfreude yet population increase is eating away at the natural world. Now the lower mandible is slipped in to cut the body away from the shell. There is panic in the streets. Yet these creatures eat with shocking voracity. Is this the direction in which we are headed?

We must ask you to remain calm and stay where you are.
As a chef it's natural to juggle six things at once yet one
need not harass a tiger to draw danger. Can we feed the
world and still have wildlife? Yet a bird of prey need not
carry off its victim and to over-claim our certainty plays a
dangerous game with public perception. Yes, but what
happens when the champagne runs out? We must continue
to demand unfettered access. Should farmers be the custodians
of wildlife? "I would have preferred him without the crocodile
tears", she said. There is also a wariness in sections of
congress. This will be key to the survival of the turtledove
yet we must ask you to remain calm and stay where you are.
One third of the population of Syria are now thought to have
left their homes.

Are we about to make the situation worse? Let's just see if we can't slip it into the conversation. I don't think there is any way we can get out safely. Yes, but do you become a one-man band because nobody else wants to play with you? Is there ecstasy in loneliness? Both are superlative swimmers and highly accomplished fishermen. Our narrative has changed. How many casualties will be caused? "It's instrumental music," she said, "all trippy doom and gloom". At this point we feel that all relevant factors should be taken into account. He became a one-man band in a state of sheer panic after his drummer disappeared just before a gig. This takes us into uncharted territory. "It's still possible to work out average intensity values for individual speech sounds", he said. Within twenty four hours most people make a complete recovery. Our narrative has changed.

"We're far more attractive to them as a source of stockpiled food," she said. It's a young male and is absolutely perfect for our management plan. When I challenged him he ran off. Why worry about what doesn't exist? We weren't expecting you until tomorrow and I just want to take another look around. In substance, the special relationship has become a euphemism for intelligence-gathering. Now our conversation can begin. Life in the water has also altered cetacean feeding habits. Incomplete, rather than inaccurate? The crocodile sank into the water and was never seen again. Fish have also been known to invade the human body in freak accidents. Now our conversation can begin.

"Do you like to loop the loop?" There's an assumption that the only people awake at this hour are truck drivers, insomniacs and mad people. Gulls and geese are already working the shore line yet this vessel descends vertically, with its cockpit near the bottom. In the early days of the occupation, the green zone played host to economic shock therapists. They create a wasteland wherever they trawl. "Concrete cutting is very sexy", she said. Did you know that many of the world's security services still preserve their most secret material on paper alone? At moments, I felt a huge wave of relief, at others a pang of incipient nostalgia. Yet he simply painted sunshine and sand again and again. These are the dwellers in the mushrooming trailer parks and this is our feeding place.

You're fairly fluent, aren't you? As record sales
collapse and record shops close, live performance
continues. It's so wonderful to be working here in
these woods. "Touring is what you make it," said Ian.
Yet we need to get to grips with the argument and
this is an emergency phone. The shoebill stork has
a massive and murderous beak. Are you an iambic
fundamentalist? It's so wonderful to be working here
in these woods. They just hold their beaks open and
wait for a fish to blunder in. Were you in the building?
Once again, the mussel has to be severed. Were you
on the same floor? Yet the only thing that separates
us is a matter of a few years. With a sensation of
stepping off a cliff I gathered my courage for the fall.

Have you seen any people being evacuated?
"I was always more interested in the ultimate
live performance rather than the recording for
its own sake," said Ian. Whatever people say
there's always a catch yet the work is hard and
the apples have to be picked by hand. We all
present an image to the world but it's too late
now – they're at the printers. "I liked the sound
of Ian Anderson, although I liked the violinist
even better, which is why I married her," said Gavin.
To begin with, we've come to a training centre
in the woods outside Geneva. Then a window
opened above him and he heard a woman calling.
A violation of international law has taken place.

On Friday night we like nothing better than shooting the breeze. Yes, but why should we play by the rules? Is this a rhetorical question? Yet the Asian hornet is on its way and the cracks are beginning to appear. Where did they come from and why are there so many of them? "The pain doesn't go away but the gaps between the pain grow longer", she said. & then there is the question of volunteers and the big society. These are the only people who have a clear motive for committing this crime. Are we arming the rebels? Lions are supposed to roar, aren't they? With respect, we've already answered that question. Books are to libraries what beds are to hospitals. We are not arming the rebels.

We remain gravely concerned about military activity.
They can crack ice a meter thick, an astounding display
of power. Yes, but are we going in? After several weeks
the dry plants are taken out from their drying sheets and
arranged on their final paper. People have often dived
with them safely but occasionally they become aggressive.
There are now more than two million refugees. What proportion
of care homes has air conditioning? We need an ecology
of sound that is more than a dense noise. Do you know
that the great horned owl achieves a wingspan of more than
four and a half feet? There are now more than two million
refugees. He seems to prefer the company of men yet most
fishermen tell whoppers. Where, incidentally, do the chemical
weapons come from? Are we going in?

"Where was your father when you left?" The last
thing you need is a rejection stamp on your passport.
We share your concerns but do we automatically
have to junk technologies that were 'of their time'?
If this idea is correct, celestial tadpoles resemble
their terrestrial namesakes. What is the science
behind reminiscence? There's a trap on the horizon
but can they see it coming? Chemical weapons
are not the first monstrous crime of this regime.
Others suffer neurological damage, deafness and
paralysis yet we surely need to focus more on the
humanitarian crisis. Somebody here is not telling
the truth and it may be time for a much broader
response. "I love my cassettes", she said.

On that last morning they assembled earlier than
usual. You can always take a trip back in time
to explore the incandescent fireball of the infant
universe. We can't pick and choose which parts
of the ecosystem we prefer yet the oracle at Delphi
was also known to take bribes. Others were trapped
in the dead-end streets and were butchered by their
pursuers. "I was watching the storm", she said, "yet
this is a fantastic pair of wheels for zipping down
the high street". Who are we to decide what the
international community should do? There were those
who couldn't keep away and those who couldn't stay.
Once again the roof will resemble a summer park yet
his finger hung in the air, pointing at nothing in particular.

III

The Manufacture of Desire

At this point the
dancer was almost
dead on her feet.
Does this action
constitute cyber-
stalking? Yet his
lukewarm reply
triggered a furious
response & the threat
of an escalation
in violence &
disorder remains.
What's the point
of lawns? Just as
important in the long
run is the issue of
reconciliation yet
each word is composed
of a separate sequence
of sounds. What's
valued isn't the quality
but the speed of your
response. Take the
sponges, for example.
Pollen levels remain
high yet you may
need to give a little
twitch after casting.
Suddenly the air is
filled with the smell
of cucumbers.

If the bird calls
little room for
error will remain.
These bunkers
give the coastal
landscape an edge
but most meat-
eaters have never
seen images like
these before.
Postcode
programming.
doesn't seem
to help the
individual
yet it's more
a question of
harassment than
invasion of privacy.
Are we using
indigenous
produce here?
Less common
is a focus on
formal education
yet the effect of
a word as sound
cannot be
separated
from its other
effects.

Where's the gun?
In another hundred
years there will be
nothing left yet these
are places where
beds of rare sea grass
provide protection
for young fish.
What sort of dress
was she wearing?
This kind of memory
is based on recollection
but she dropped out
of school a year later
to pursue a career
in acting. "Googling
yourself is a highly
treacherous activity",
he said. This was a
new feeling for me,
disconcerting in
its virulence, but
immediately after
the election freedom
of speech is closed
down. A lovely sea breeze
is all we really want
yet the mystery remains
a mystery & this is
not a court of law.

What is the future of street food?
The alligator gauges its prey by
height but there's a preserved-in-
aspic feel to this immaculately
clean town centre. Is the idea of
ethical capitalism a contradiction
in terms? Today we're having chips
& egg with lots of bread & butter.
At sea, flying fish have been known
to strike sailors but anyone who goes
out to protest is likely to be shot.
"I'm going to put my cards on the
table", he said. There's a lot here we
don't recognise yet it's all about
economic growth, with the environment
coming a poor second. How long do
we get for lunch? Fiction, by contrast
is despised & public spaces are being
freed-up to allow more food traders into
the city. Swimming at the site is banned
yet ushers are giving hand signals to
indicate the number & location of seats.
Is this the spirit of the marketplace?
Many treatment methods are now available
to the stutterer yet average earnings are
failing to keep pace with price rises.
Does street food have to mean 'fast-food'?
"None of this is easy and you can still see
the tensions playing out", he said.

If it's too easy
to map influence
then the work will
probably be dull.
Yes, but is this
simply the death
rattle of the old
politics? They tend
to be written from
left to right, with
the symbols generally
facing the beginning
of a row. What is
in question here is
not memory but
free reproduction.
Will the lights stay on?
Yet he remembered
virtually nothing of
his everyday life & this
lake is still filled with
trout. A sound sensation
may remain unchanged
in tone, volume &
intensity. Are you an
optimist or an aggressive
pessimist? Everything
here seems impossibly
small. Frequently, his
examples are bizarre
yet nothing in my
experience feels quite
like a live snake. Is
Bournemouth your kind
of oyster?

As you can probably see
we've moved location yet
there are a lot of small fish
out on the surface & there's
a high risk of localised flooding.
Are we looking at a pre-emptive
strike? Somebody must be
targeting us both but why
have you decided to speak
about this in public? At its core,
branding is about vigorously
controlled one-way messages.
Put in these terms, his work
sounds narrow & repetitive,
but somebody is always stealing
something & what turns our
brains on is often a sense of risk.
"I'm a long way from being a
shambling wreck", he said.
Are you a candidate for the
deputy leadership? When going
to such lengths a reliable camera
is essential yet they also use
the surface film as a means of
communication. Yes, but what
about my obligation to my sources?
For the first time the special
relationship looks in serious
danger yet we're obsessed with
power & the fact that we haven't
got any. These days the job
comes with a lighthouse.

Last night he dreamed
that he was swimming
underwater. We are definitely
at the beginning of the
end of this story as the
drama is heightened &
everything is pushed to
the limit. A great horned
owl moves silently over
my head & the air is suddenly
full of hideous smell.
When he was acting he
thrust a snarling intensity
at the camera. A giant squid
has just left & retreats into
a world of darkness. If you're
not impressed by its size,
consider its other adornments.
What's happening below the
surface is more important yet
it made no sound, even in that
crisp medium. "Arrogance
allied to ignorance – terrifying,
isn't it?" Why threaten the witness?
Little wonder that they live
for the day yet its components
are durable & the quality is
outstanding.

What are these
performances but
contemporary art
rituals? In a circus
tent the scene is
quite surreal yet it
was decades before
she encountered
another cougar in
the wild. Is there
an alternative to
the mass, cultural
art of consumerism?
He soon found
himself alone at
dusk, searching for
another building.
Yet this is not a
message about
rebellion & such
handicaps are more
properly called
syndromes. Is there
any water in the trough?
"Performance art
often has a subject
but no object", said
Laurie. I felt a great
wave of happiness
at the same time, a
desire to run towards
the light.

Despite my
reservations
this dish is
irresistible.
On the floor
of life the
commodity
is money yet
none of this
is feasible
while there
is armed
resistance.
"We also
need to find
subjects who
are prepared
to cooperate",
she said. From
an early age
she was left
to her own
devices yet
poets with an
understanding
of history are
often filled
with a deep
foreboding.
Suddenly,
power has
moved from
the universities
to the students.

Most listeners, when
asked if there were
any sounds missing,
said 'no'. Our focus
is on the first round
though there must be
some concern about
the selection process
& the bait is never
taken with a rush.
How do we go about
changing our cognitive
map? Participants
sample & swap
recipes for around
an hour and then place
their bids. These are
the teenage feelings
that you have yet each
word has a particular
meaning & minutes
later we're on the
road again. Can you
find me a swan mussel,
please? Imagine you
have a problem on a
ship. Who do you
complain to? Yet his
pattern-cutting is
masterly and it's really
all about the lever
in your arm.

Eating
punctuates
boredom.
Yet he could
not imagine
the future
any more
than he could
remember
the past.
How strong
is your
argument?
Each click
is like a dim
camera flash
yet we lured
them in, using
the promise
of free chips.
Everything
around us
is lush &
green.
Has the
village been
untouched by
the recession?
Yet actors
playing the
parts of suspects
do strange things
& may be taken
on any kind
of natural bait.

"It's a strange & potent
thought to have about
another planet", he said.
What on earth is a sepia
memory? "With respect,
sir, we all make mistakes".
Yet our sense of self includes
our stories of our past &
where we think we're going.
What if we look at the
difference between rhetoric
& reality. When most of us
were growing up the solar
system seemed reliable &
well-behaved yet for these
reasons we need to realise
that robots may be more
effective as supervisors than
as slaves. "I suppose that's
why I finally snapped", he said.
Perhaps we should talk
about the idea of crime as
entertainment. Yet these
pieces echo minimalist
sculpture while also bringing
a threatening vibe to the space.
In the case of the mass media
the issues are somewhat
different but how do we then
join up the dots in our own lives?
"You need to get the words
into your mouth", he said.

After all these years
his personality still
eludes me. The chiaroscuro
is diffuse, the accents
dissipated, yet this is
a heavy duty museum
& the feelings came & went
instantly. In connected
speech, very different
processes seem to be
in operation. Did you
notice anyone else in
the vicinity? Our panel
is expected to release a
final decision tomorrow
yet this is not a story
which shows any sign
of going away. Where
did you learn all those
words? What is needed
now is a more detailed
identification of the
problem areas. As the tide
came in the battleship
passed out of view. "I no
longer hear the voices",
he said. We will move
into the area as soon as
our briefing is completed.

It would be foolish not
to take precautions yet
this is not how the dream
is supposed to die. A six-
second video may be easy
to shoot but it takes thought
& ingenuity to tell a story
in that time. Why are you
playing so hard to get?
A clear distinction needs
to be drawn between sign
language & gesture yet
decisions have to be made
on other grounds. Some
aquatic animals cultivate
poison as a defence, while
some choke to death from
ambitious feeding. "You're
about as convincing as a
collective, corporate hug",
she said. We should also
note at this point that the
brain uses our two ears in
different ways. Another
perfect day has come to an
end yet she has a reputation
for being a straight talker
& backup arrives just in time.
Scepticism, I quickly learned,
is not considered an asset in
the low-wage service sector.

There is, of course, no
such thing as the effect
of a word or sound, yet
filming underwater presents
us with many practical
challenges. Who will
actually secure the chemical
weapon stocks? Yet the
activists have taught some
lessons of their own &
these people have learned
to steer clear of charismatic
leaders. Meanwhile, remote,
exotic destinations have
become easier to get to.
"You know I've always
been a capable gamekeeper",
he said. There remains a
lack of research in this area
yet its claws are absurdly
muscular & this fish has
probably never seen a hook.
Then she was introduced to
an older friend with a flashy
car. Neither was serious &
the engagement was broken
off by mutual agreement.
I had barely put on my
coat when I got another call.

A small head in the water
will not be seen. It was an
eerie & moving experience.
She was so totally still that
I wondered for a second if
she was breathing. "If you've
got good friends around you,
you can rebuild your life", she
said. Have we got time to read
the newspapers? She was experimental
before her time. These smaller,
targeted movements are clearly
part of a common cause. Yet my
pet hissing cockroach poses no
such risk. His breathing is
strained & he is sweating to
the point of dehydration. It was
an eerie & moving experience.
Here we have a media house
of mirrors when what we all
need are more windows on the
world. Yet our hard hats are
discarded & she also has to
rewrite parts of the instrumentation.
When he was released, seven
years later, the world was a
different place. It was an eerie
& moving experience & I put my
whole strength to the gate & pushed.

Life at sea has
changed dramatically.
"We may have
to do the wrong
thing for the right
reason", she said.
How much does
the idea that they
are to blame, remain?
Yet it's still just a
ditch in the desert
& street-wear has always
been something of
a renegade movement.
"One ear may have
an advantage over
the other", she said.
Mostly, the victims
are taken while fishing
or filling water vessels
yet people see their
movements as a means
of escape. These are
now available in a
rainbow of colours
from classic green to
racy red. We are not
yet in the danger zone
but pirates are already
affecting our passage.

He took to roaming the
house at odd hours, always
at a loose end. Wherever
we have travelled, the rat
has come too. Little by
little, his physical posture
improves. Some of them
are careless with their teeth
yet they have a prodigious
reproduction rate & ground-
nesting birds are often the first
to suffer. Are you working on
another page-turner? "It's this
interaction between species that
is most important", he said.
Simple signing systems are found
in a wide range of professions
but there remains a blurring
between the internal & the external
worlds. "Humility is a key virtue",
she said, "& in no way do we know
what we're doing with planet earth".
Yet the first step in the reception
of speech takes place when sound
waves arrive at the ear. A collision
becomes more serious when the
fish is well-armed, although it
inhabits deep water & rarely
encounters surfers & swimmers.

It may not be a
criminal offence
but we need an
alternative system
of classification.
"Singing bossa nova
is a bit like being
on the crest of a
wave", she sang.
How easy will it
be to get this gas
out of the ground?
At one extreme, this
handicap may be
quite mild yet another
food skill is coming
into play. Do you
get a real kick out
of numbers? These
were dark, windowless
places which shut
out the sun. Engaging
but rarely elating,
this show doesn't
quite produce the
required sugar-rush.
Yet the 'real world'
is not a place we
regularly inhabit
& many musicians
remain in exile.

One way to understand
human behaviour is to
study its counterpart in
animals. "These people
need to be made accountable",
she said. Yet we all once
had a practical skill that
connected us with our food.
His expectations, on the
other hand, were wildly
off the mark. Are you
full of vim? With few
exceptions there is no
narrative framework yet
physiologically & biologically
they are identical. Both
men said they didn't take
drugs knowingly & are
assisting us with our
enquiries. "We've taken a
step forward by using rats",
she said, yet he's from the
'less is more' school of
acting & spent three years
working in a kitchen when
he left college. Is this the kind
of interactive learning that
your programme plans to
introduce? If all research
projects were judged on 'pay-
back' criteria, important
work would never get done.

IV

Bandits

Do you get on with your neighbours?
Here we have a new kind of creature
with no moral dimension. These are
mostly slender, fast-moving snakes
but some rob individually while others
work in pairs. An additional battery is
available. In return you will receive
an enhanced compensation package
yet this silent war over whose lives
are counted long predates September
the eleventh. Technically, the charges
are invalid. Yes, but is he a proto-
revolutionary or a bandit? Turpin
arrives masked and armed with pistols.

If we allow nature to create a natural
equilibrium it will take care of our
coastlines. There remains the problem
of how the rioting spread yet horse theft
was a capital offence and punishable
by death. It's time once more for the
William Tell Overture. "I'm just trying
to get a sense of the shape of the place",
she said. Listen out for the nightingale,
the chattering reed and the sedge warbler.
For these men the hope of reprieve seemed
a slim one yet this is now the most common
account of the death of Robin Hood.
The world of fish is rich with weapons.

Mounted robbers are widely considered
to be superior to footpads but the crocodile
waited beneath the tree throughout the
evening. "We could always reverse all of
the above", she said. The origins of Tonto's
horse, Scout, is less clear yet a study of
errors is important because it shows children
breaking fresh grammatical ground. When
the eight-year war finally came to an end
only the arms merchants were unhappy.
Her sudden calm was not capitulation yet
all audiences want to be entertained and
confusion was evident from the outset.
These birds are wanderers of the open oceans.

In all the recorded accounts, Robin's
meeting with the friar has a water motif.
Yet the short-drop method meant that those
executed were killed by slow strangulation.
Meanwhile, in the absence of ice these
huge animals are forced to take to land.
Am I interrupting? After breeding they
disperse widely and many follow the squid
and fish shoals into the north Atlantic.
Yet our earliest literature is studded with
celestial dreams and the bandit appears to
be a pre-political phenomenon. Yes, but
are we simply getting harder to scare?
Who was that masked man?

He awoke early from sleep, his head full
of bad dreams. Naturally, the scene produced
its own music yet they usually choose areas
of heath or woodland for their criminal acts.
Eventually the roots make contact with the earth.
These were wage riots and attacks on threshing
machines. It's important to keep an eye out for
extreme behaviour yet the Lone Ranger is never
seen without his mask or disguise. Such advice is
rarely given and in ancient cultures the dream
was largely seen as a visitation. Yet the faces
come back and are replaced by more faces.
Social banditry of this kind is one of the most
universal phenomena known to history.

There is of course an easier place to ascend.
What these forms of banditry share in common
is that they tend to balloon in times of economic
crisis. Who is going to stand in as temporary
manager? These changes will happen regardless
of future emissions yet they rightly felt that
they had little to hide and that public opinion
is on their side. "There is no better education
than having to fight for your future", said Owen.
Why doesn't the economics of bacon stack up?
A shout sounds out in the silence of the night
yet this type of outlaw usually travels and robs
by horse. He climbs a ladder to the gallows and
speaks to his executioner.

I turned briefly in my seat before vowing never
to look back. Suddenly, the peace is disrupted by
the sharp crack of a rifle. Bandits are, by definition,
plugged into market networks but you can always
return with us now to the thrilling days of yesteryear.
Light reflects off an Italian marble staircase yet all
apartments are served by an underground carpark.
Once again, the threshing machines become the main
target. Volatility here seems close to disturbance and
intervention may still be possible. Some confusion
about the protesters' political agenda is understandable.
Yet here, at least, it was wages and not machines that
appears to have been the sole issue. Cats, on the other
hand, still think like wild hunters.

Are you like a Lone Ranger figure, blazing
your own trail? Yet we are all free to
ransack the museums of our collective pasts.
On our first morning, a local friend offered
to take us to a cave at the other end of the
island. It may be that the shortest distance
between two points turns out to be a curve.
Two of these disturbances were minor affairs
yet the manner of Robin Hood's death
deserves consideration and many of these
artists are also incredible innovators. Other
sects show a similar pattern and modern forms
of organisation will need to be absorbed.
Maybe we should all become a one-man band.

Like it or not, when the future arrives, you are going to need a lawyer. Such accidents tend to be brushed over in science fiction yet our sun is travelling through much stormier skies than we thought. Were these labourers relatively prosperous or were they among the poorest of the poor? Many of us find this issue very challenging yet wildcats probably moved in to exploit this new resource. So much for international policing and global control. There are villages with epidemics of incendiarism and there is also a homoerotic element. Welcome to the future – a legal minefield. Yet we never quite reveal what these terms might be.

We may now begin to draw a provisional profile of the village disposed to riot. On the guitar, this has the effect of increasing and then lowering string tension. Fish of any size are incredibly difficult to study, yet to our eyes, glass looks like a solid, while at the molecular level it behaves like a liquid. Who needs a rocket when you can use a balloon? Live lobsters glare at you from the glass tanks. Even so, they remain aloof and inscrutable. Specific sites linked to the outlaw include the Robin Hood Well and the Major Oak Tree. Everything about this fish is designed to make it a top predator.

Conditions are ideal, especially after
all this rain. Yes, but how exactly can
a water rat masquerade as a snake?
Although there was no evidence to
suggest that Turpin was directly involved
in the thefts, he was a close associate
of the gang. Have you ever felt the urge
to perform works of charity? Social
banditry has next to no organisation
or ideology yet the two men were aware
of her, as the magnet that had brought
them together. "Visual signals, however,
have their limitations as advertisements",
she said.

As the pressure drops with altitude, the balloon expands until it finally bursts. “It’s hard to say what it means to be human any more”, she said. Yet this relationship between the ordinary peasant and the rebel outlaw is what makes social banditry so significant. On the guitar, vibrato has a dampening effect, causing the note to decay faster. In the string theory multiverse, anything you want to happen can happen if you pick the appropriate universe. Such an approach is never politically neutral yet hook a big sea trout at night and you’re in for an epic fight.

It's not simply a question of how we
can understand the future but how can
we make sense of the present? "Carnal
pleasures will do nicely from now on",
he said. Cats and humans go back a long
way but what exactly is the origin of
Tonto's horse? In some of these encounters,
issues other than tithes and wages were
raised by the rioting labourers. Yet your
presentation may be light-hearted or esoteric.
She is also the perfect travelling companion,
poised and well-tempered. Occasionally, a
technology comes along that is so disruptive
it changes everything.

V

Moving in the Right Direction

When the tape is played back, the process is reversed,
reducing the hiss. "Yes, but I'm just trying to get
a sense of the shape of the place", she said.

To be an inventor you have to live with uncertainty.
Approaching dusk is a key feeding time yet you can
always replace a chunky brogue with a chunky heel.

Potential losers fight a great deal harder than potential
winners. However, the anxieties about luxury never
really go away and we've had a right old result today.

"We are simply damaging ourselves by what we are
doing to others", she said, "but I can't handle this
amount of information and there's no room for finesse".

In theory, you can impart more energy to the
string with vibrato yet it was incredibly hot and
both soldiers were carrying heavy backpacks.

Do you have unanswered questions which keep you
awake at night? Everything has to happen in a single
breath yet clams can live for hundreds of years.

Our mudflats also supply less tangible services yet its
adipose fin is clipped to aid identity. "The workforce and
its terms and conditions will have to be slashed", he said.

Users may also reply to your posts. At this point the
counting of the money began. Yet these are incremental
developments, not bold leaps into the future.

This was a dangerous time, when
the paranoia in the pirates began.

When did you last cut the mustard? There's too
much efficiency around here yet he's not a fanatic,
he just wants people to get out on their bikes.

What do you do when you're in the dark and the
demons come? The moment of crisis is judged to
have passed. Then we started a term of disorder.

Yes, but what about the elite athletes? Another was
hunkered flat, as though wishing he could disappear into
the ground. The verdict itself is expected to come quickly.

This confrontation is in a long list of incidents yet
investment income is significantly down and it's
usually the weather that puts a spanner in the works.

"You really need to get into shape for that kind of duty",
she said. Can we watch too much comedy? Excess is not
a problem but this event has been advertised in advance.

Even rats can enjoy a good laugh. Later in the meeting, talk
turned to a more comfortable question. Who was that masked
man? I made him a cup of tea and sent him on his way.

"There's a common assumption that the academy is a
privileged space", she said. Yet the idea of the public realm
is in eclipse and with it a conception of civilization.

What was it that prompted your interest in understanding
laughter? It's a good time to take a music break. Parrots
may mimic us but only robots can say something original.

When did you last cut the mustard? It's usually
the weather that puts a spanner in the works.

He stood there in the doorway, staring at me with
those bright, piercing eyes. "Have you ever seen a
fat berg?" Before I could answer he was on his way.

These figures are based on too small a sample and
are little better than guesswork. Yet the bees are only
defending their hive against a perceived threat.

All around us there are furious people. "Gambling
doesn't dominate my life any more", he said. At least,
this is what I told her too and I think she believed it.

It's not the business of the botanist to eradicate
the weeds yet there is no claim of responsibility
for the ambush and further action will be required.

It looks like we're going to need a change. Yes, but
why did the scientific method take so long to emerge?
After a while, she heard footsteps coming down the stairs.

"No matter what I've done you've always been there to
rubbish it", she said. Now the ministry of defence is recruiting
voluntary specialists to create a protective force in cyberspace.

There was a sudden impact, almost like being in a bumper
car. Butter-baked cod falls apart in luscious flakes yet
we don't all have access to a microphone and an audience.

Do you have a phobia of beards? It's just that this apartment is
so aware of itself. Oh, so that's why you wear the mask. This is
where we end up when basic needs are treated as commodities.

"You have a very selective memory", she said. Seconds
later there was a loud bang on the window next to our table.

Is that the bacon cooking, by any chance? He
smiled at me without animosity yet as a child
he must have known these streets back to front.

Chickpeas, apparently, don't like rain. Do we
know what the time-frame is? Back on the beach
I picked my way over pieces of loose driftwood.

Are you sure you didn't hear the shots? Yet there's
an immediate cash payment followed by a long-term
payback. Do you ever fall prey to impulse purchasing?

It had never occurred to him that he would be
required to take questions from the floor. As the
whale dives its flukes are angled towards the canyon.

There's still very little light on the forest floor yet
people with this condition have to develop a thick
skin. He finished his coffee in silence then rose to go.

On certain sultry days the rudd go into a frenzy of
incautious feeding. Equally surprising is a very low
admission fee. Yes, but have you found your inner bird?

Where is this voice coming from? Yet the older you
get the more you are who you are. She discovered an
awareness of light that she hadn't previously appreciated.

Changing this to the 'cloudy' setting will result in much
warmer and more natural colours. "I wish politicians
would stop talking about hard-working families", she said.

What is involved here is the idea that
the vote continues to carry authority.

When do we start playing the game? It's an exercise in
artifice yet these people are always looking for an identity.
This became a dominant theme in the narrative about her.

You've got to have fun with this or it will drive you
nuts. What exactly do you have in mind and will it
work? "At least my conscience will be clear", she said.

In reality, both approaches have problems. There is
gravity though and sometimes exotic matter collapses
into black holes. We should stay within the barricades.

Each side blamed the other for the economic malaise
yet what we need now is planning and organisation.
Who isn't fascinated by the sea and what it contains?

Somewhere in a conference room the money was
being arranged. It was a strongly-worded statement
yet what you really need in a wildlife garden is diversity.

Here we have a squirting cucumber. You can make
them as small or as large as you wish but others
are able to remain alive for astonishing periods.

Is consumerism the greatest device anyone has invented
for controlling people? Others are able to remain alive
for astonishing periods yet many more are lost at sea.

"We can't comment on the status of individual cases but
there's no doubt we're having a massive impact on the cull",
she said. Now we can hear the greater-spotted woodpecker.

Our situation is becoming an impossible one.
How many can you print in a day?

We are actively exploring the air above distant worlds,
searching their skies for signs that something is at home.
Perhaps we should resist the temptation to wallow in sacrifice?

"I knew this could be a sound of the future", he said,
"yet the answer is quite simple – weed growth". Let us
all count ourselves lucky if we wake tomorrow morning.

"I don't want Shakespeare, I just want schlock", she said.
When did you last see a wrinkly tomato on a supermarket shelf?
Moments after the siren sounds, the tenement comes to life.

He knew that he was being unreasonable but he no longer
cared. It took only fifteen minutes for the approach to become
an attack yet the science behind the cull is controversial.

Because they're shy, nocturnal birds, you'd be hard pushed
to see them in daylight. "We need people to make our chutneys",
she said. There is, of course, an easier place to ascend.

Standing made his head spin and he was lucky to reach the
bed before he toppled over. As a climber gets near a canopy it
expands its leaves. Other models are surely worth considering.

This is a bruiser of a main course, a fish dish for people who
crave meat. Back then cycling was a rather relaxed affair yet
here and there a wall stands up out of the debris.

As it happens, the destruction could have been worse yet you need
to search for that ideal mix of close-up and distance shot. Bizarrely,
in this limited space, some works are in multiple versions.

Moments after the siren sounds, the tenement comes to life.
All of a sudden the border was open, just like that.

A glum conviction was starting to take shape in her mind. Meanwhile, on the so-called 'safe islands', unemployment is rampant. Drill a little deeper and the results are fascinating.

It doesn't do to discuss such matters over the phone. There are some beautiful things in the sky yet this has not stopped a tidal wave of takeovers and mergers. Was Robin Hood Welsh?

Although they suggest animals or plants, these works are not identifiable as anything real. Are we losing the right to be forgotten? "It looks like a melon but it's slightly longer", she said.

We may have to switch to 'catch and release'. This was a time when the forest was being eroded from within, yet we want to know what lived there, how it evolved and what it ate.

Amateurs make a big contribution to astronomy but there's another much-used term here – sustainable development. Slowly but surely he slid surreptitiously towards that forbidden pleasure.

This plant is commonly known and easily seen. Hence the hint of apple with citrus flavours. Yet the venom in its sting has no purpose other than deterrence. Cooling engines tick as the hysteria subsides.

Word soon spread of its extraordinary acoustic properties. "We are trying to discover the role that tides play in the behaviour of sharks", she said. On hearing this story, the Lone Ranger reveals his real i.d.

It's a method better used in summer on small rivers with not much flow. Meanwhile, we're doing what we can to limit supply. "Mary Poppins is the story of a failed family", she said.

When a star moves towards us, its light subtly shifts towards the blue end of the visible-light spectrum.

A shout sounds out in the silence of the night. What does an athlete need to do to compete successfully? These are people who have never been on the shop floor in their lives.

Am I being fitted up? Others have been attacked after moving over a hive yet in such a bare acoustic performance it's hard to judge how much he's moved on musically.

"Travelling slowly completely changes the way your mind works", she said. It was lucky that I didn't need a bed or a mattress. Elsewhere, it will be cloudy with outbreaks of rain.

Suddenly there was a large thud then the lights went out. The cat permitted her caress for a second before darting away into the drawing room. Cataract surgery may also improve sleep patterns.

Do you know anything about a planned rebellion? Gradually, some of the listeners broke away from the crowd. "No, but I've been a seaside entertainer for over thirty years", he said.

As we have seen, it's unlikely that global politics will solve global warming but Bowie's approach to his art has always been influenced by books. Our story continues tomorrow.

Are you a consummate master of language? Counting sunspots is not as easy as it sounds. Whether you like it or not is beside the point. At other times, new inventions prompt new legislation.

When he re-emerged, rubbish was piled high in the streets. Clearly, some secrets are still worth keeping. Yet it's hard to judge where theft ends and inspiration begins.

Are we creating money out of thin air? There are many around here who relish these succulent leaves.

Are you an activist or a journalist? Of course, he may simply pull the trigger and go for a down-the-line glory shot. "I can't find any evidence of bribery", she said. A cold wind blows over the hills.

Your hook should be kept sharp and clean. You can't be specific using this procedure, yet the mouth of a grouper is built to engulf its victims. Approaching dusk is a key feeding time.

Street slang is all around us. You know we're not supposed to let you just wander off but this makes for a faster, more productive session. Whatever happens, it is ease of use that will win out.

"It's good to have a new convert", she said. Groups of bluefish sometimes feed in a shark-style frenzy. Many responded by funding the resistance with what little revenue they had left.

We're in the first hour of a very delicate situation. It's not just dead sharks that we're interested in but the best strategy may be to prevent the spores from germinating. Suddenly it all makes sense.

What could have brought that on, do you think? In some places, cats may actually help diversity by killing rats. It's a bit windy and that's going to cause problems. Over time, any such resistance diminishes.

What you are hearing is not a change in pitch but a change in volume. "We're looking for about seventy pounds of fish", he said. How they love to go for these marginal rushes.

You can always listen to the hum of a healthy engine. "She's a wonderful talker and I love talking to her", she said. This may be a lucky break for softer, smaller species, lurking in the sandy seabed.

"How long have you been a bee inspector", she asked. These are night creatures and they are in search of food.

"We're looking for something that is very small, very cold and very dim", she said. You can tell that these people are in distress. Within minutes a huge crowd of supporters filled the square.

Some academics are appalled by his approach to the subject but we're struggling here to keep control of the group. Not the least important agent in plant distribution is man.

It's been suggested that people are using food banks because there are now more of them. Yet there's always been a mystery attached to pike fishing. Shadows waver and sway from every doorway.

Regulation always runs behind the technology. Naturally, the envelope has also disappeared, yet this species can be very skulking, while its large size makes it appear clumsier than smaller warblers.

Did he punch the air as an expression of selflessness? "None of these images are available online", she said. The song swelled in a great burst of emotion and then died. How do we find our own voice?

There is a real sense of warmth and the tell-tale buzz of gentle, happy conversation. Yet territory is all-important to cats, which might go some way to explaining their inscrutable behaviour.

Why is there something, rather than nothing? Who says that bathroom scales have to be white rather than silver? Yet we never actually see the planet – it's all done by inference.

How important is the moon in all of this? Both sides are to blame but the root of the problem is a republican party that is losing touch with reality. Yes, but what can you bring to the table?

Most owners stroke their cats
simply because it gives them pleasure.

As in many campaigns the publicity stunts used to promote a
cause often run counter to their supposed aims. Academic studies
of art and popular music sit alongside classic 20th century novels.

Immediately the road deteriorated and we entered a vast shanty
town of shacks with corrugated roofs. "It's part of my vernacular",
he said. It will be a long time before these treatments become a reality.

Eventually, there will be a reconfiguration, yet this was never
going to present a reasonable way out of their difficulties.
This weed is full of wriggling creatures of all shapes and sizes.

Many responded by funding the resistance with what little revenue
they had left. Yet this is really useful for tricky lighting situations.
On migration they are most often found in low trees, bushes and scrub.

All of this rain is going to bring the rivers up, yet a purring
cat may also be hungry or mildly anxious. The exhibition's
audio guide features an interview with David Bowie.

While his behaviour was boorish his barbs were unbelievably
funny. Both sides sealed their agreement. You could have a large
planet, surrounded by rocky moons, and these could be habitable.

We were all expected to enter 'not-guilty' pleas. Approaching
dusk is a key feeding time yet this is the most potent venom so
far discovered in a snake. This ward is known as the 'sleep room'.

"Let them talk – we've done nothing wrong". She writes about night
in a dream language with a heavy use of multi-lingual puns. This
is one of the world's biggest oil producers, yet poverty is rife.

Shadows waver and sway from every doorway.
As they come closer we begin to relax.

www.ingramcontent.com/pod-product-compliance
Ingram Content Group UK Ltd.
Pitfield, Milton Keynes, MK11 3LW, UK
UKHW040558210726
13854UKWH00008B/1467